My Pet Crocodile

My Pet

Crocodile

Slightly
and Other Outrageous Verse

Verse by John Billings
Illustrations by Janette Todd

Chokecherry Press
Bountiful, Utah

First Edition

10 9 8 7 6 5 4 3 2 1

Library of Congress Catalog Card Number: 93-72718

Publisher's Cataloging in Publication Data
Billings, John.
My Pet Crocodile and Other Slightly Outrageous Verse
p.   cm.
Summary: An illustrated collection of humorous and
whimsical verse on a variety of subjects.
ISBN 1-884035-55-8
1. Children's poetry, American.   [1. American poetry.
2. Humorous poetry.]   I. Todd, Janette (date) ill.
II. Title   1994
811'.54—dc20   93-72718

To Megan, Clinton, Nichole, Jeffrey, Jeremy and Elizabeth

My Pet Crocodile

My pet crocodile
is wearing a smile,
like there's something
he knows I don't know.
Where are Sammy and Sue
and Timothy too?
They were here
just a moment ago.

I have this terrible feeling
my croc's not appealing,
and for me
to obey zoning laws,
I should trade for a puppy
or a goldfish or guppy,
or something with
less formidable jaws!

Bug Off!

Our neighbor's baby seems to be
a connoisseur who's learning.
He has strong likes and dislikes too,
he's really quite discerning.
He popped a striped crawley bug
into his mouth one day.
He tasted it, savored it,
then swallowed it away.
The only one who seemed upset
was the little fellow's mother;
she yelled and screamed and scolded him—
he shrugged and ate another!

Mural Girl

My little sister's into art
with innate talents to impart;
a master of the colored crayon,
pencils bright and paints that spray-on.
Her latest gallery is in our hall
and mom can't scrub it off the wall.

Bye-bye Fly

G lider spider
spins a web
of silky thread transparent—
to catch a fly
should it try
to go where it should daren't.

Gravity Cavity

Thrill-seeking Sam leapt off the bridge
secured by cords of bungee.
The cords stretched out but lost their snap…

Sam hopes the ground is spongy.

Wet Pet

What a remarkable animal, my pet goat!
    Just look at the garbage he stuffs down his throat.
With the great quantites of trash
he is able to stash,
in deep water he sinks, unable to float!

Hover Cover

Why do humming birds hum?
Aren't they more talented birds?
I think they're probably just like me
and they forgot the words.

My Brother is a Grouch

My brother is a surly grouch,
that's all that I can say.
He grumbles when I wear his clothes
or don't put his toys away.
And I don't know why, this morning,
he's in such a sulky snit.
I brushed the dog's teeth with his brush,
but I took proper care of it.

Stick Shtick

Jake Slakes was afraid of snakes,
he regarded them with loathing.
"They've got scaly skin from tail to chin
and writhe naked with no clothing."

Jake Slakes was afraid of snakes.
He walked through the woods with care,
so he wouldn't miss any warning hiss
that would tell him snakes were there.

Jake Slakes was afraid of snakes,
and one fateful day while hiking
went into a dither, seeing one slither,
which wasn't at all to his liking.

Jake Slakes was afraid of snakes.
He picked up a stick, you see
—to bash it — to thrash it,
he thought snakes were his enemy.

Jake Slakes was afraid of snakes.
What relief was his when he found
it wasn't a snake that made him shake,
—it was only a stick on the ground.

Jake Slakes was afraid of snakes
and the stick in his hand gave him reason.
The stick was a snake— and it swallowed Jake!—
('though snake-haters were then out of season.)

Skule Bored

Jeremy Jarvis couldn't stand school,
education just wasn't his bag.
He measured his success out during recess,
playing dodge ball, hopscotch and tag.

Try as they may, or at least so they say,
his teachers could not seem to reach him.
Readin', 'ritin' and 'rithmetic
were all things they just couldn't teach him.

Years have gone past—he's grown up at last
and his stock has certainly soared:
He owns his own business, is frightfully rich
and presides at the local school board.

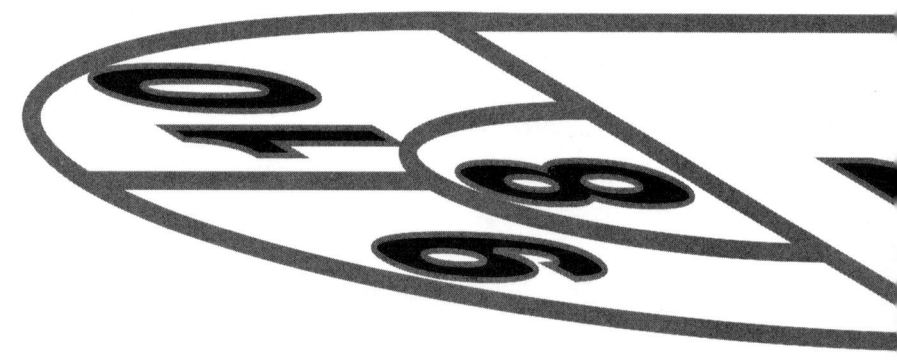

Main Pain

Cowboy Cal from Albuquerque
was sort of strange and kind of quirky.
He rode his horse through weather murky—
and ate canned beans and stale beef jerky.

He recited poems of Western lore.
A ten-gallon hat was what he wore
upon his head and nothing more,
then wondered why he got saddle sore.

He rode all night, he rode all day—
and sang cowboy songs along the way.
Why he did it I can't say,
but he stopped singing at Santa Fe.

I don't know what that trip taught him,
but the horse had fleas and old Cal caught 'em.
Beneath his hat, he scratched and fought 'em,
he was one sore cowboy– from top to bottom!

Cal soon retired and now doesn't ride.
It was not because of his sore hide
that hurt so badly he could have cried—
But what hurt most was damaged pride.

If you're ever in the Old Southwest
and see a cowboy all brightly dressed,
it could be Cal, as you might have guessed,
he'll not be riding, he'll be at rest.

You're now enlightened— as bright as day,
and it matters not what others say—
You know the **real** reason— hey—!
why bow-legged cowboys walk that way!

Feet Feat

Consider the duck:
Its feet are flat.
(It waddles a lot
because of that.)

Camel Riding

Dromedary, Bactrian—
the choice is up to you.
Do you take your camel
with one hump or two?

Horrid Harvest

David Dodd is rather odd,
    his manners somewhat crude.
Potato vines grow from his head
and his finger tips are chewed.

I asked him how he got that way
—he seemed a curious sort—
He coughed a little, moved some leaves,
and this was his retort:

"My mother often cautioned me,
and plainly did assert
if I didn't keep my ears washed clean,
plants would take root in the dirt.
And she warned that if my fingers
kept picking at my nose,
nose-dwellers would attack and make
me wish I'd used my toes."

"As you can plainly see, my friend,
I've suffered through the years.
My fingers have been chewed to bits
and green vines grow from my ears.
But although those may be tragedies,
things are better than they sound,
'cause when it's time to reap the spuds
I get ten cents a pound!"

Tough Torts

Did you ever try to eat a hippopotamus?
Or gnaw and nibble on a kangaroo?
The meal would last from May on through November
with all those patties, chops and stew!

And when dealing with exotic kind—
especially wild hippopotamuses,
always keep foremost in mind
they really are quite ornery cusses!

So don't ever eat a hippopotamus
or dine on kicking kangaroo—
'cause kangaroos get tough and stubborn
and hippopotami get worse— they sue!!

Crinkle Wrinkle

When skinny Winnie takes a bath
she soaks in suds 'til noon;
and even though her skin comes clean,
it wrinkles like a prune.

When Winnie's washed and feeling new
and unadulterated,
she doesn't look so scrubbed as much
as she looks corrugated.

Self-Help

Some call him a human corkscrew
—the circus contortionist.
He seems to bend and twist around
from his ankle to his wrist.
Because in all directions
his extremities do point,
I'm sure his entire body
is completely out of joint.

He gives "bending over backwards"
a new meaning without doubt,
and if it's ever praise he needs,
he'll never do without.
For if, in fact, an "atta-boy"
is what he seems to lack,
he can twist-up like a pretzel
and pat himself upon his back!

Rubbernecker

She walks so very gracefully
with her head up in the trees,
'though her legs are rather spindly
and knobby are her knees.
I really like the tall giraffe
down at the city zoo.
I accept her as she is
and I think she likes *me* too.

Summer Hummer

The honey bee— she has two ends:
 With one among the flowers she fends,
and gathers nectar moist and sweet,
then produces honey good to eat.

At the rear of her's her other end
which she uses to defend
her hive, her honey, everything—
So treat her right or feel the sting!

Dental Hygiene

Grandma Johnson brushes her teeth,
she does it every day.
She makes them bright and sparkly
then puts the brush away.

The only time she fails to brush them,
(and it gives her grief),
is when she finds the brush, but then
she just can't find her teeth.

Chicken Scratches

Chicken in the fryer,
chicken in the pan,
I'd take chicken anytime
and anyway I can.

Chicken fried and
chicken baked,
chicken salad with
chicken flaked,
chicken scaloppine
chicken cordon bleu,
chicken cacciatore,
chicken, I love you.

Croquettes are great or
chicken pie,
and à la king?
—for that I'd die!

The only kind of chicken
this little discourse knocks
is the kind I have right now:
I *hate* the chicken pox!

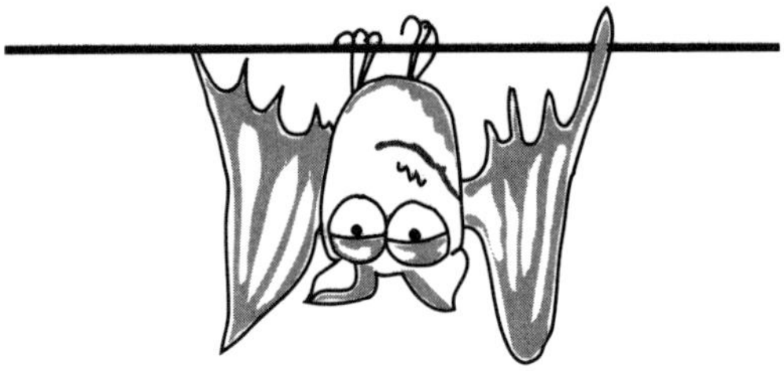

That's Bats

A bat in flight is quite erratic,
with herky-jerks it's never static.
I don't like bats, and that's emphatic!
(especially when they're in our attic.)

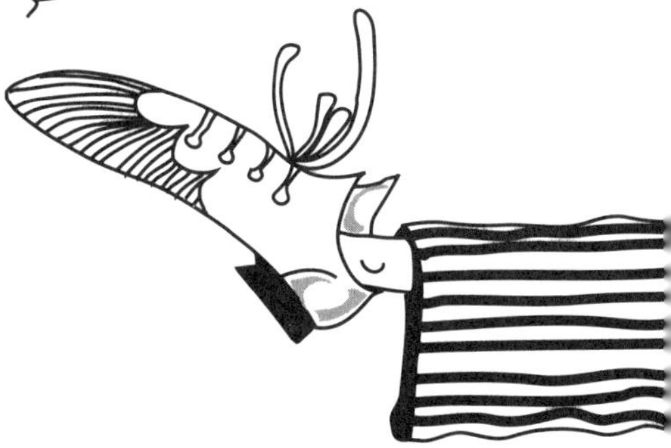

Mad Dad

My dad is on a rampage,
he just kicked the dog.
I saw him trip on something green,
then he threw out my pet frog.

I heard him cuss and use a word
to help him try to cope—
I know that if **I** said it
my mouth'd be washed with soap.

I hate to see him stomp and shout
and carry on that way.
He is normally kind-natured
and has but good to say.

But every year is just the same
and no one here relaxes—
on the fifteenth of April we steer clear—
the day dad computes his taxes.

Slugfest

One slow-moving slug met another
   in the middle of the garden one day.
Each slow-moving slug thought the other
should hasten to get out of its way.

But it's not in a slug's nature to hasten,
so each patiently took its sweet time
and eschewed any merit in racin',
for to ooze slowly in slime seemed sublime.

Null Pull

Lots of things are kept in drawers,
there are shirts and shorts and sox.
Most drawers slide open easily,
some are closed with keys and locks.
Some are full of knives and forks
and others tape and string.
There are even other special drawers
where you could find 'most anything.
But whenever I need something
you know it's just my luck—
it is always in the drawer
that I can never get unstuck.

My Brother, the Computer Whiz

M y brother's into high-tech.
At computers he's a whiz.
It's really not surprising,
it's just the way he is.
He likes to hear the disk drives whirr
and see the screen shine bright,
and when he's crunching numbers
he is really quite a sight.
It's the same when typing words—
he never bends his knees.
In fact, he stands on tiptoes
just to reach the keys.
I don't think that's strange at all,
I really don't, do you?
After all, my brother's tall
for one who's only two!

Puppy Love

My dog is a stupendous, spectacular beast,
intelligent and noble, to say the least.
Spot knows every trick in the dog-trick book,
and I've taught him to clean and even to cook.
There's not a thing cleaner than the floor of my room,
he's a bona fide miracle at the end of a broom.
Whenever I'm hungry and for food I am looking,
Spot truly excels in the art of French cooking.
He'll attempt any job with a wagging tail,
you can count on Spot; he'll never fail.
He will stay with a task right to the end,
I don't know about "man", but he's *my* best friend!

Sinister Seafood

Rapscallionish scallops,
criminal clams,
miscreant mackeral,
and abalone flim-flams,

Scalawag shrimp
and sinner swordfish,
crooked king crab,
scoundrel squid that go "squish,"

Unsavory soles
and larcenous lobsters,
halibut heavies
and tunafish mobsters,

Haddock blackguards
and reprobate oysters,
pink prawn punks
that you won't find in cloisters—

You must admit
that this litany is sad,
for there is nothing worse
than seafood gone bad.

Trod Bod

Mr. Cockroach, Mr. Cockroach,
why do you scurry so fast?
Your kind have been here for many a year—
Are you afraid you may be the last?

If you come close, I'll have to admit
that I have a foreboding hunch
the last sound that you hear when you come near
may be a sickening, audible CRUNCH!

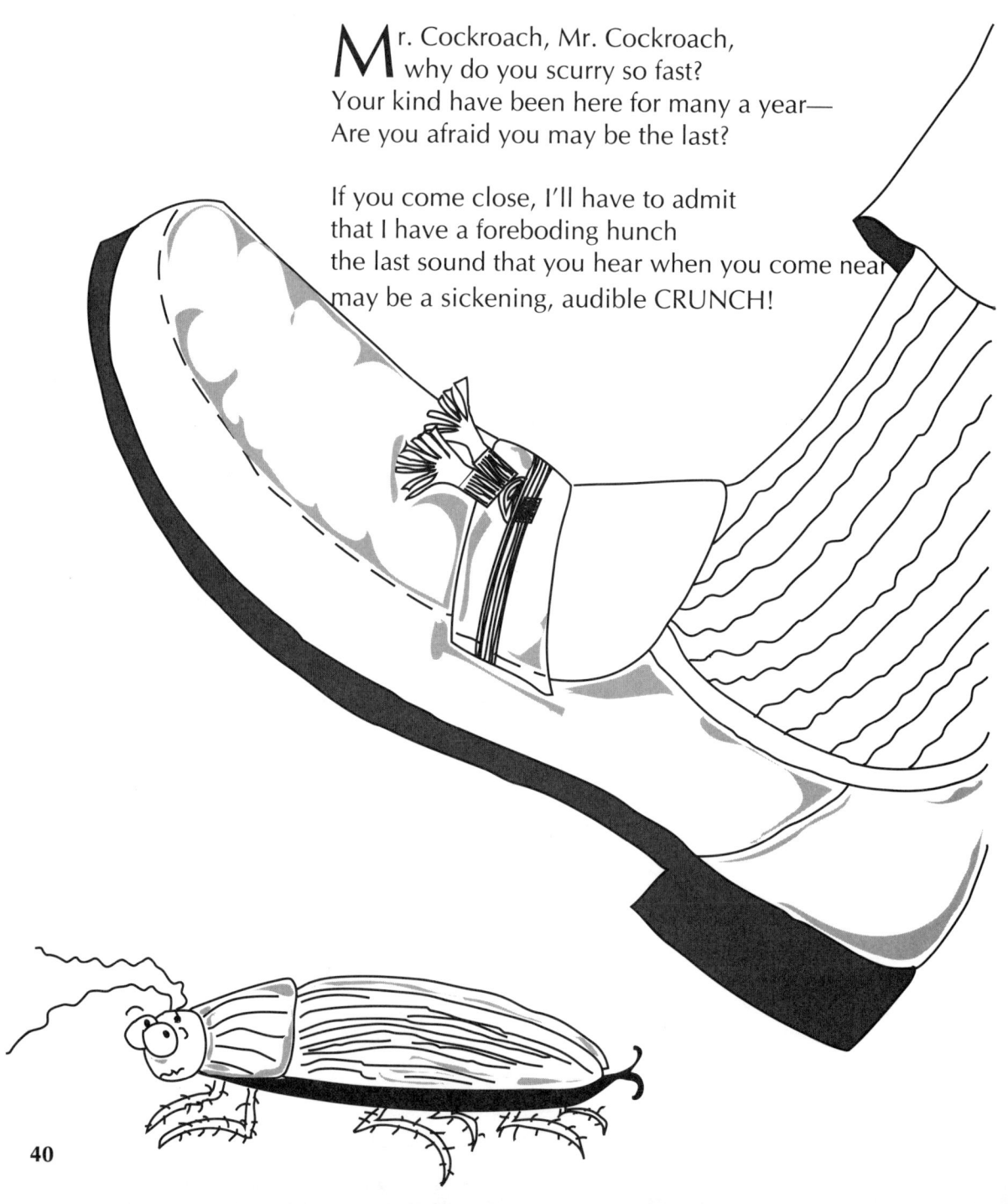

Peas, Please

José Manuel Gallegos
wouldn't eat his peas.
He shoved them up the kitty's nose
and squashed them with his knees.
He hid them in the ivy plant
in a white ceramic pot,
he made pea-mush of some of them,
but eat them he would not!
He squished them through his fingers
and wiped them in his hair—
José Manuel Gallegos
really didn't care.

Vicious Vegetable

My mother seems to love it.
She says it's good for me.
Some famous folk disdain it, and
I don't blame them: it's broccoli!

I cannot stand the smell of it
while it's cooking in a pot
—nor the thought nor taste of it
either cold or steamy hot.

I'm certain that this vegetable
is a dark conspiracy
of intergalactic aliens
who wish us harm, you see.

So let's all band together,
and fight for all we're worth.
If we won't eat our broccoli
perhaps we'll save the earth!

IFO's

Barnaby Brown did not see
tiny men whose skin was green,
but an actual flying saucer
he can swear that he has seen.

He noticed that it whizzed on by him
as he was looking up,
it was followed by some angry words
and a swiftly flying cup!

Headless Hank

Headless Hank stomped off to school
—his cap was always skewed.
Without a head Hank was a fool,
he acted rough and rude.

He argued loudly, made crude sounds;
he was a loutish boor.
His bad behavior knew no bounds,
Hank seemed rotten to his core.

But Hank changed his ways at once
when a classmate to him said,
"Hank, stop acting like a dunce
or you will never get ahead!"

Bad Actor

Horrible Horace Hanover
used to cut up in class every day.
He would show off, throw spitwads and wisecrack,
just to hear what people would say.

Horace was a great entertainer,
at least that's what he thought.
He kept his classmates in stitches,
while believing he'd never get caught.

He thought his acting was great—really first rate,
but hadn't counted on the critic's review—
When the report came out, what a terrible pan:
—Scholarship "F", Deportment a "U!"

Squeezer Geezer

Octopus,
   Octopus—
slippery, stealthy octopus—
With eight limbs you have your charms,
but which are legs and which are arms?
I can imagine that each tentacle
as a squeezer is quite "unrelentable."
So as a squeezee, I'll avoid the fuss
and stay far away from you,
Mr. Octopus.

Abrasion Invasion

Floyd flew on his skateboard with flair and aplomb,
but he didn't wear pads, and that proved to be dumb.
He acrobatically "-boarded" with three jumps and a spin;
now the *pavement* has more than *he* has of his skin.

Eye Opener

Chocolate-mint cornflakes,
  strawberry mush,
french-fried omlettes,
goat's milk slush,
prune-juice fizz
and toasted ham,
with pickle-butter
and sauerkraut jam,
carameled eggs
that crunch when you chew,
I love breakfast—
how about you?

Steel Meal

Samuel S. Oliver, the side-show sword swallower
swallowed twenty-two swords in a row.
When he was done, he found just twenty-one—
now where did that other sword go?

"It's not in its scabbard," Sam nervously jabbered,
"it's really a mystery to me.
I ate twenty-two, so now what do I do?
I'm just glad I didn't eat twenty-three!"

Sam pondered and thought to where that sword might have got;
it was time that proved well-invested.
"Eureka!," he chirped, as he belched and he burped,
"It's certain that sword's been digested!"

Impression Obsession

Johnny picked the time and place,
it was a grade-school dance.
Then Johnny picked the girl to ask—
it was his first romance.

Johnny picked the clothes he wore—
a clean, white shirt just pressed.
He picked a tie, his pants and socks—
John was neatly dressed.

Johnny picked the moment;
he seemed so debonair,
as he approached his lady,
out of place was not one hair.

Johnny picked his way before her,
(he had picked for her a rose).
But Johnny ruined the whole effect
when Johnny picked his nose!

Spit-Splat

The archerfish! What a marksman of note!
—and such a good shot, it has reason to gloat.
   For you can be sure that it'll
   hit every bug that it shoots with its spittle
then swallow as much as its tummy can tote.

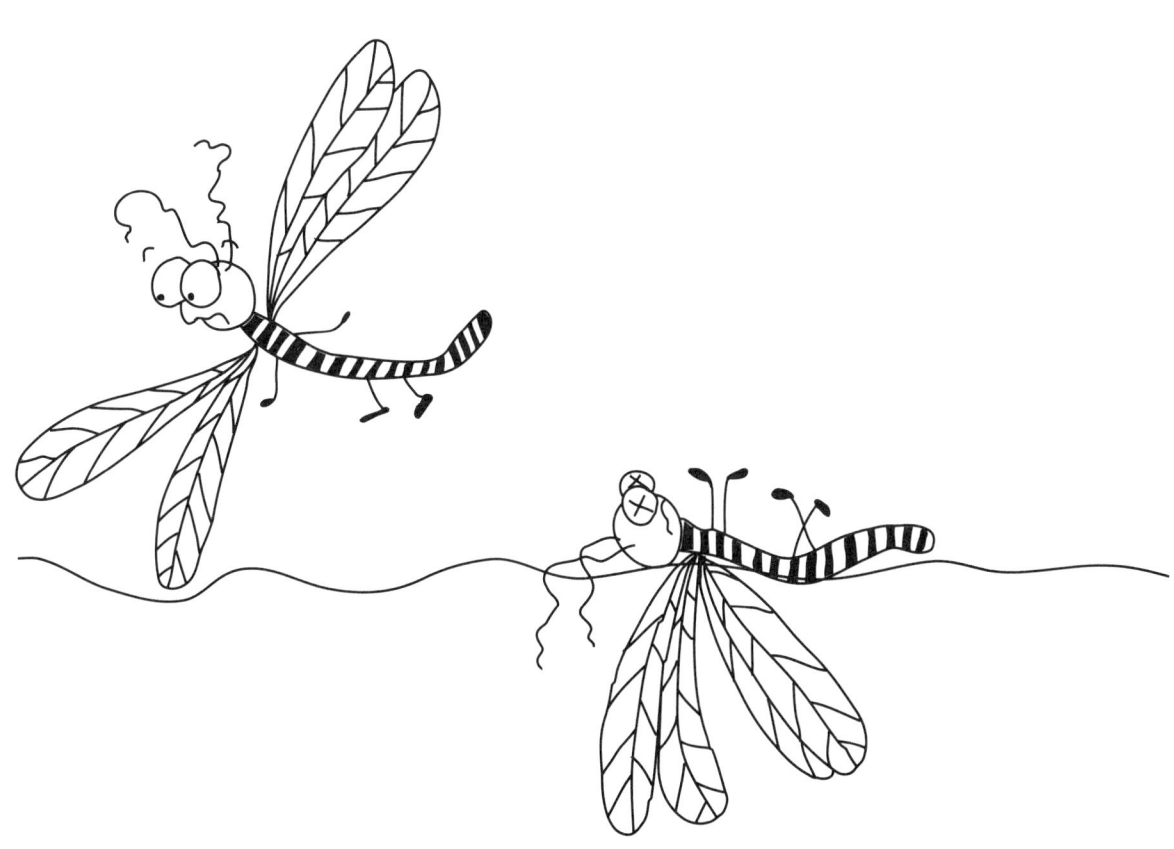

Playtime

I like to play with lizards.
I like to play with frogs.
I like to play with things you find
under rocks and under logs.

I like to play with the guys next door;
we're a rough and tumble lot.
I like to play with tanks and trucks
or whatever toys they've got.

I like to play high in the trees
where climbing takes some skill
—but any rough-house, rugged fun
will usually fill the bill.

I do not like not many things:
bows, and lace and pearls.
But least of all, I do not like
to play with other girls.

Bruise News

Polly Pritcher pinched her sister;
  Polly's sister pinched her back.
Where they pinched they are not telling,
but what once was pink is now blue and black.

Jump Grump

Gerald jumped off the garage roof
with an opened umbrella in hand.
He thought he'd glide slowly to earth
and light like a feather he'd land.

Gerald's knowledge of physics was lacking,
his descent wasn't slow—it was fast.
Now Gerald can ponder the science of flight
as he heals in a full body cast.

Just Desserts

My sister swiped my special pie—
the one that I just made.
I'd put it out to cool it off
there in the playhouse shade.

She ate it all– the whole darn thing,
I hope she's feeling well.
Whether indigestion strikes her down
is something time will tell.

I know that when she swallowed it,
it landed with a thud,
'cause it wasn't baked with lucious fruit—
it was completely made of mud.

Prediction Depiction

I'm Weatherbee the Weatherman,
predicting weather as none else can
and telling whether there'll be weather, man,
'cause I'm Weatherbee the Weatherman.

I'm Weatherbee the Weatherman.
I hardly ever blunder.
If I predict that it will rain,
it rains with force and thunder.

There *is* none better—I'm the master.
I'm a peachy-keen forecaster,
forecasting every storm disaster
with its broken glass and falling plaster.

I predict those storms at night
that seem so dark and frightening—
the ones with rain and hail and wind
and flashes of blue lightning.

The only time I've ever erred
and completely missed the call
was when I predicted there would be
no weather—*none at all!*

I'm Weatherbee the Weatherman.

The Magic Dimple

Suzanna Anna Jones
has a dimple in her cheek
that she uses quite effectively
to ward off mama's pique.
When she spills her milk, or throws her toys,
or pulls the doggy's tail,
she gives that little smile of hers,
and you can bet that without fail
that dimple works its magic,
and with the sparkle in her eye,
reduces mama's anger
to a wistful little sigh.

Suzanna Anna Jones
has a dimple in her cheek,
and when daddy's careworn world
is starting to look bleak,
she climbs upon his knee
with "sticky" on her hands and "dirty" on her face,
grins up that little dimple
and things fall magically in place.

Suzanna Anna Jones—
a soul so innocent and simple,
and everybody knows by now,
there's magic in that dimple.

Smile Wile

John Edward Williams is a busy little man,
he scurries through the house like no other toddler can.
He only stops to twist the knobs of Daddy's TV set
or push the buttons on the phone—no shout has stopped him yet.
He turns the light switch off and on, it seems a great delight,
and he never tires of it, he does it day and night.
John Edward Williams has a silly little grin,
a smile that melts your heart away and brings the sunshine in.
When he breaks his mother's vase or mars the table top,
he smiles that silly smile of his—there's no way to make him stop,
and anger flees replaced by awe and just a little shame;
when John Edward comes into your life things are never quite the same.
—And 'though you may be burdened by troubles pressing in,
those troubles seem much lighter when John Edward grins his grin.

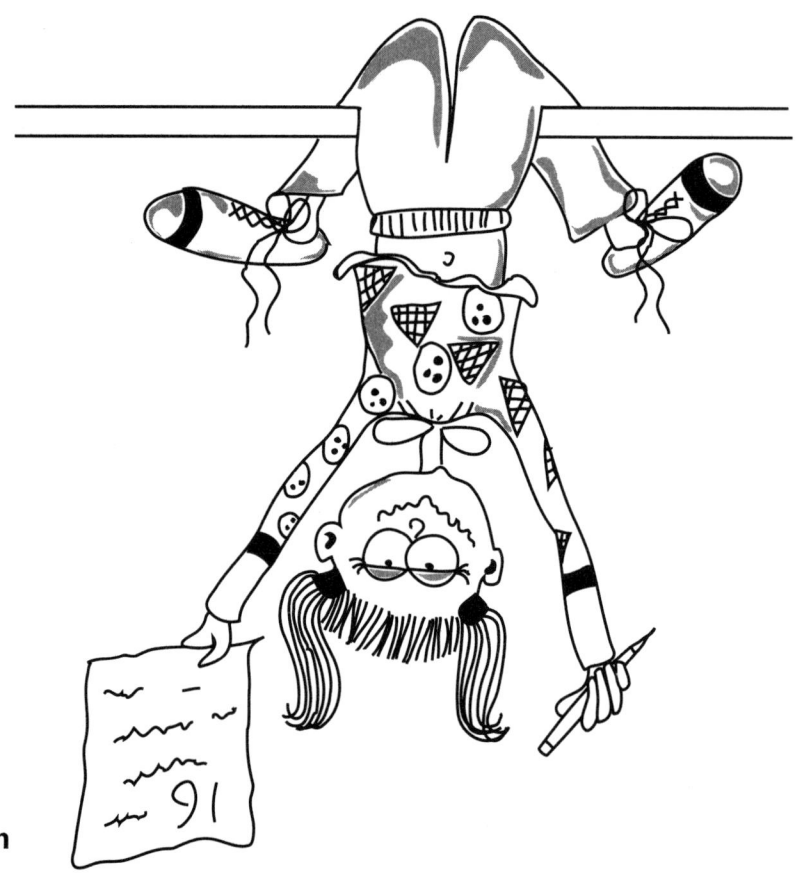

Brain Drain

Imelda Elizabeth Francine Brown
does her homework hanging upside down.

"This way the blood goes to my brain
and super-intelligence I seem to gain!
Just look at this score from my last test.
Since it's the highest, I must be best!"

I hated to tell her, but she just hadn't seen
that the 91 she boasted of was really just 16!

Night Light

Firefly, it's not your nose
that makes you my kind friend.
No, my summer evening glows
When you're lighting your *hind* end.

Smooth and Chunky

Crunch crunch crunch time, munch time, lunch time;
my friend Ralph is not the least bit thin.
I blame that on peanut butter, some of
which Ralph has all over his chin.

I think it really sticks to his ribs,
but not according to Ralph:
"Ah know id doesn't stick to mah wibs,
'cause id's stickin' to da woov uv mah mouf!"

Thick
-n-
sticky

Art Start

My cousin Karen is great with paint,
she has a crisp, creative flair.
She can apply it with the finest brush
or spray it lightly through the air.

At times she smears the goop on thick
with a short, dull-bladed knife
and expertise so keen you'd think
she'd done it all her life.

Her color schemes are striking,
her textures all unique
and when she paints a face, that face
might be considered classic Greek.

But Aunt Kate becomes upset
when Karen paints like she is able.
It's 'cause Karen's used her mother's stuff
at her mother's dressing table.

But Karen takes such wrath in stride,
and copes quite well with it:
"I'm going to save my money," says she,
"and buy my very own make-up kit!"

Wild Child

We never take Roger to the zoo anymore;
the reasons are patently clear.
For Roger to be an arm's length from the cages
is for Roger an arm's length too near.

The last time we took him, he clambered on in
with the monkeys and short-tailed macaques.
He swiped all their food and ate their bananas
and suffered their random attacks.

He declared himself king and swung through the trees;
the monkeys stared at him with awe.
The last time we saw them, they were all feeding *him!*
He waved to us bye-bye, ta-ta.

We never take Roger to the zoo anymore,
indeed, there is no need to do so—
for Roger remained there and proposed to a bear
who is busily preparing her trousseau.

Theologic Logic

From dust we came, the Good Book says,
and we shall return to dust.
It seems to me a bit bizarre,
but if we must, we must.
I checked the space beneath my bed
and had a thought that's numbing—
I'm sure that in that quiet place
someone's going or someone's coming.

Snack Attack

Jimmy ate a caterpillar.
His brother made him do it.
He made him put it in his mouth
and then he made him chew it.

But Jimmy spoiled his brother's fun,
you might have guessed he would.
He looked his brother in the eye
and said, "that tasted *good!*"

M is for...

Moms can be an awful drag.
    You may know what I mean—
they way they talk and things they say
are practically obscene.
Things like "eat your vegetables,"
and "turn off the TV set,"
"Shut the door!" "Put on your coat—
it isn't summer yet!"

It seems they're always telling you
just how you should behave.
It might even be called comical
how much they rant and rave:
"Change your clothes and wash your face—
be sure to comb your hair."
"Do your chores and homework
or you can't go anywhere!"

"Take a bath and go to bed,"
"Turn down that radio—"
"Turn off those lights and get to sleep!"
are phrases many know.
"Excuse yourself!" or "drink your milk"
"Please don't pick your nose."
"Make your bed," "clean up your room."
And on and on it goes.

Moms can be an awful drag,
or so some kids might whine.
But I know a *perfect* mom,
And luckily she's *mine!*

Attention Suspension

Tyler J. Sailson couldn't sit still,
his mouth he couldn't keep quiet.
His teacher arrived at the end of her rope,
thought of mayhem, even thought she might try it.

"I have spent hour after hour unselfishly working
in out-of-classtime preparation,
to teach, to instruct, to inform these kids
and to provide them with some inspiration."

"But that boy understands not a thing that I say,
his attention span spans not a minute.
What I'd like to have now, besides tape and a gag,
is a straight jacket with Tyler strapped in it!"

Tyler was the cause of each classroom disturbance.
He was the center of each perturbation.
And when he missed class or was absent at all
it produced in his teacher elation.

Years have passed by, and nothing has changed;
his behavior still sticks in her craw.
Tyler grew-up and married her daughter,
and pays no attention to his mother-in-law.

Snob Stopper

Snooty Samantha Cicily Smith
walked with her nose in the air,
Concerned with Samantha Cicily Smith;
for others she had not a care.

Continuing to walk with her nose elevated,
out in the weather so brisk,
exposing two nostrils to all of outdoors,
carried with it a definite risk.

Misfortune befell Samantha Cicily Smith
with her nose pointed up to the sky.
The two holes attracted a hornet, a hawk,
a sapsucking woodpecker and purple horsefly.

What they did when they dove she will not say;
if you ask Samantha, she'll merely mumble—
But one thing to me is easy to see:
now Miss Smith is a whole lot more humble!

Screaming Yellow Honker

The kids tell scary stories,
  but they don't frighten me,
although it's as big a monster
as you might ever see.
If you look hard near the corner,
you still can see its track.
It was here only this morning
and likely will be back.
It's roar is like a lion's,
like a tiger it is dressed,
mostly brilliant yellow
with black trim for the rest.
It makes a stop for kids each day
and opens up its mouth,
devours them all,
then turns the corner heading south!
But it doesn't frighten me
and I won't make a fuss,
for next year will be *my* turn
to ride the school bus!

Slow Go

I want a sloth for a pet.
I could keep up the pace
of a sloth in a race
so never behind would I get.

A sloth's not like a cheetah or horse;
its pace is agonizingly slow.
No need for a workout on a race course,
for got-up and gone is its get-up and go.

A stroll in the park could last the day through;
in fact, I think that's what I need.
I want a sloth for a pet, oh yes I do;
they may not be cuddly, but a sloth's just my speed!

Soapless Opera

Gertrude Grime is not sublime,
she isn't even pretty.
Gert loves dirt and dirt loves Gert—
that's known throughout the city.

Dust swirls about her in the wind,
her visibility drops to zero.
Don't try to penetrate that cloud,
filth would cling to any hero.

She leaves tracks wherever she goes;
in winter when she walks downtown,
the footprints she leaves in the snows
are stained a dirty brown.

In springtime when it rains and rains
and rivers start to flood,
Gertrude Grime does *not* come clean,
—the dirt just turns to **Mud**!

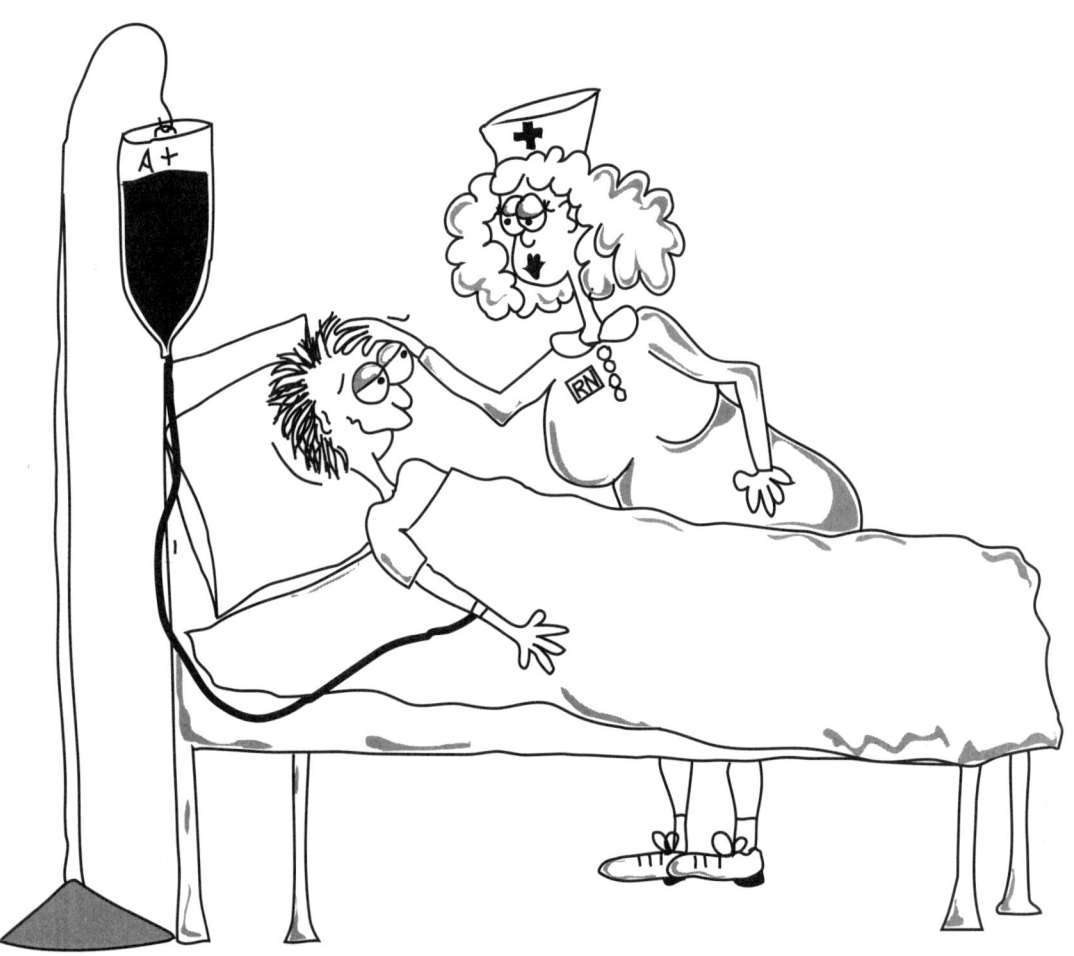

Dry Guy

A humongous mosquito, the size of Toledo,
bit Bob on the back of the arm.
It left an infernal itch, the irritation of which
could have caused Robert irreparable harm.

He scratched it then rubbed it, then ignored it and snubbed it,
but that itch just would not subside.
He thought his circulation might fail, and grew dizzy and pale
contemplating that hole in his hide.

"The only solution for that insect's intrusion
is to put back what that bug took away."
He reached this conclusion: "I need a transfusion!"
So he got one—*ten gallons* they say.

Rope Hope

*T*wenty-two gazillion and one—
Louella Penelope Green,
—*Twenty-two gazillion and two—*
she's a rope jumping queen.

—Twenty-two gazillion and three—
She's the playground's best,
—Twenty-two gazillion and four—
she never stops for a rest.

—Twenty-two gazillion and five—
Look at her jump so high;
—Twenty-two gazillion and six—
that girl can really fly!

Louella Penelope Green,
she makes me really burn.
—I just wish she'd miss for once,
so I can have a turn!

(*—Twenty-two gazillion and seven—*)

Winter

My nose is froze and brightly glows,
it runs and drips and sneezes.
Does my frosty breath forebode my death?
—It comes in gasps and wheezes.

Some say ice is nice
and winter's fun;
but I much prefer
the summer sun.

Summer

I feel beat with prickly heat,
my face with sweat is dripping.
Will I expire as I perspire?
—Through my mind dark thoughts are zipping.

Some like the heat, the sun's bright glare;
but if I might be so bold,
I'd trade it all for just one day
of refreshing winter's cold.

The Chupadek

The chupadek plocked soggolite
and wrapt the wogglebee.
The crattlegong fritched up the shank
and crinched for all to see.

The blotzenfelter ran amok,
a sight the flagle frant.
The sadic sorple sang a song—
a demonic charking chant.

With callen fleeped and taver still,
an eerie scruper bore
the pain of twenty torkels,
and grivel granced once more.

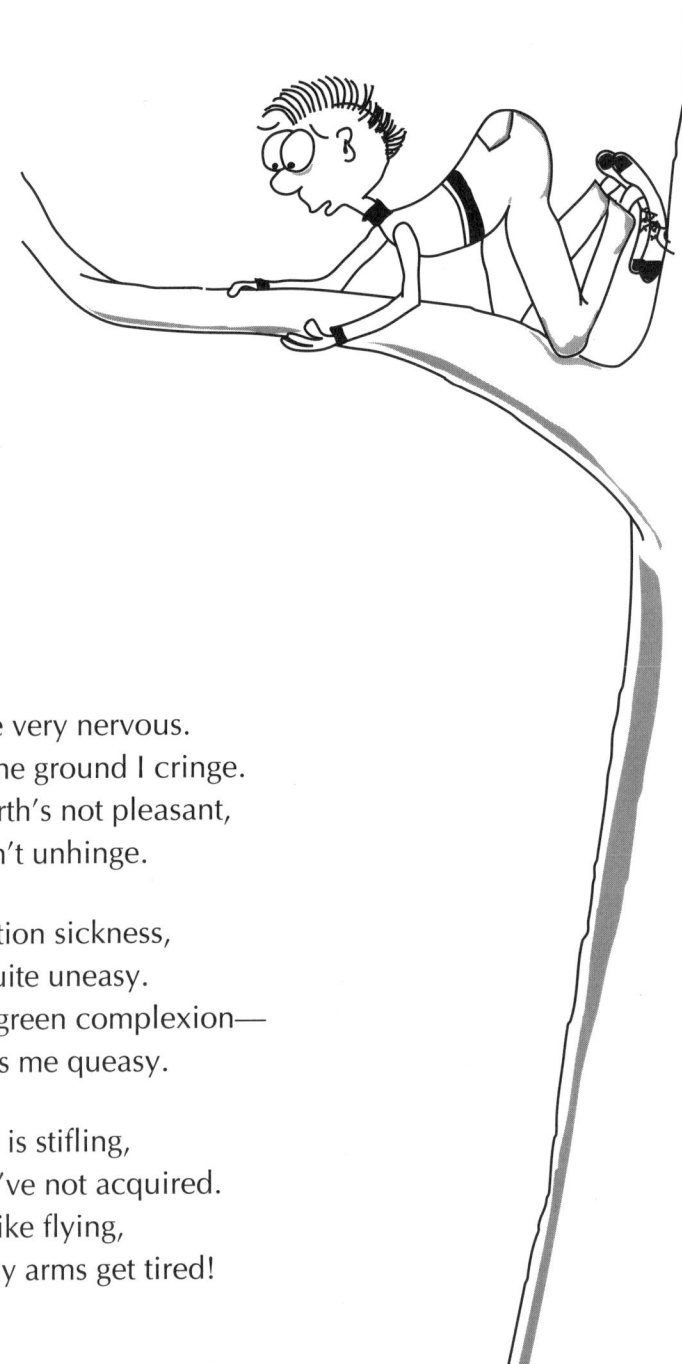

Sorer Soarer

Flying makes me very nervous.
When I leave the ground I cringe.
Leaving Mother Earth's not pleasant,
the wonder is I don't unhinge.

I'm a cinch for motion sickness,
flying leaves me quite uneasy.
I turn a pale, then green complexion—
when I fly, it makes me queasy.

When I fly the fear is stifling,
a calm assurance I've not acquired.
No, I really don't like flying,
and worst of all, my arms get tired!

Chatter Matter

My older sister likes to talk,
she's full of yakity-yak.
My ears are wilted from the noise,
I'm afraid they may soon crack.

Her mouth's motor must be huge,
I'm sure that it's bodacious
to make my sister as she is:
incessantly loquacious.

An interruption could slip a cog
of anyone so garrulous,
but someone ought to stop her
even though it might be perilous.

I think there is a cure for her—
perhaps a Velcro gripper,
or an operation to implant
a stainless-steel lip zipper!

Grandma's Cookies

I like them hot, I like them crisp,
I like them soft and chewy.
I like them round, I like them fresh
with chocolate chips so gooey.

I like the taste, I like the smell
that fills my grandma's kitchen.
To gobble down those cookies good
is for what I'm really itchin'.

Chocolate chip and ginger snaps—
They all pass the test.
All grandma's cookies are just great,
but I like the *dough* the best!

Fish Wish?

I caught a fish and it was big!
It almost broke my fishing rig.
It fought and fought and thrashed about,
the largest of its species, there is no doubt.
I can't begin to say how large—
that fish I caught from off the barge.
My arms just won't stretch far enough
to indicate its length and stuff.
I only know I caught it, but I'm sad to say
before I pulled it in the barge, that huge fish got away!

Mean Mean

Sarah Slat is extremely fat,
her sister Sal's so slender.
Their Uncle Hank is gruff and mean
and Aunt Alice much too tender.
Grandpa Slat is bent and ugly,
Grandma's straight and fair—
her graying tresses drag on the ground,
Grandpa's bald without a hair.

Sarah's father, Mr. Slat,
wears the biggest smile in town.
But Mrs. Slat is often seen
with her mouth formed in a frown.
Cousin Kevin towers Six-Foot-Seven.
Sarah's brother is Five-Foot-Short.
After surveying the entire family,
I have this announcement to report:
Looking at them one by one
they do present a sight,
but when lumped together, I would say,
that on the **AVERAGE**, *they're just right!*

Ant Rant

When I'm at home with my ant farm,
I could watch ants by the hour.
Being so superior
gives me feelings of great power.

Ants can lift ten times their weight,
they display an intellect too.
They live sociable, civilized lives—
there's not much an ant can't do.

When we're on a picnic
ants lose their fascination.
I don't know who invited them,
they seem an infestation.

And I have one worry
perhaps we should discuss:
on a picnic when we're not watching them,
I think *they're watching us!*

Some Gum!

Darryl Crumm loved bubble gum,
he chewed it every day.
He blew a bubble that proved trouble:
it exploded blowing everything away.

When that bubble failed poor Darryl sailed
high up into the sky.
He was bound to hit the ground
unless he learned to fly.

Darryl Crumm chewed that gum
and blew for all his worth.
He blew quick and soon a hot-air balloon
and floated softly back to earth.

Damp Tramp

I have new shoes, they're really keen.
They turn me into a jumping machine.
I can jump most anything around,
with new shoes on it only takes one bound.

There are rain-puddles here, and I don't want to get
my brand-new shoes either moist or wet.
So I won't jump those puddles wide
that have shoe-magnets hidden deep inside.

Wading in puddles would surely be fun,
but I should stay far away 'til they've dried-up in the sun.
I may be too close— Help!—and like a flash
the shoe-magnets have got me!— SPLASH, SPLASH, SPLASH!

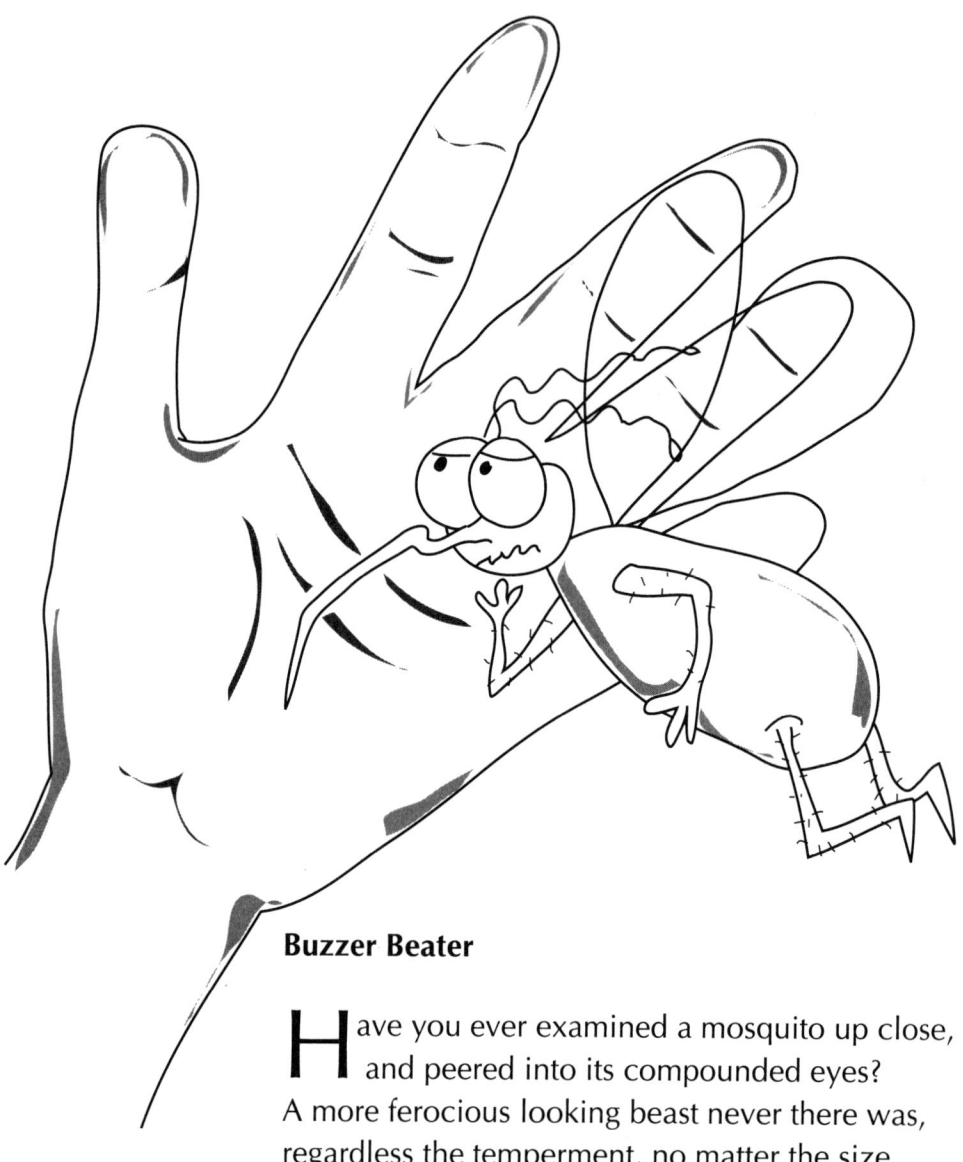

Buzzer Beater

Have you ever examined a mosquito up close,
and peered into its compounded eyes?
A more ferocious looking beast never there was,
regardless the temperment, no matter the size.

The mosquito possesses an arsenal of tools
for cutting and drilling in skin.
It takes but a moment after setting up shop
to have its blood-drawing stick stuck right in.

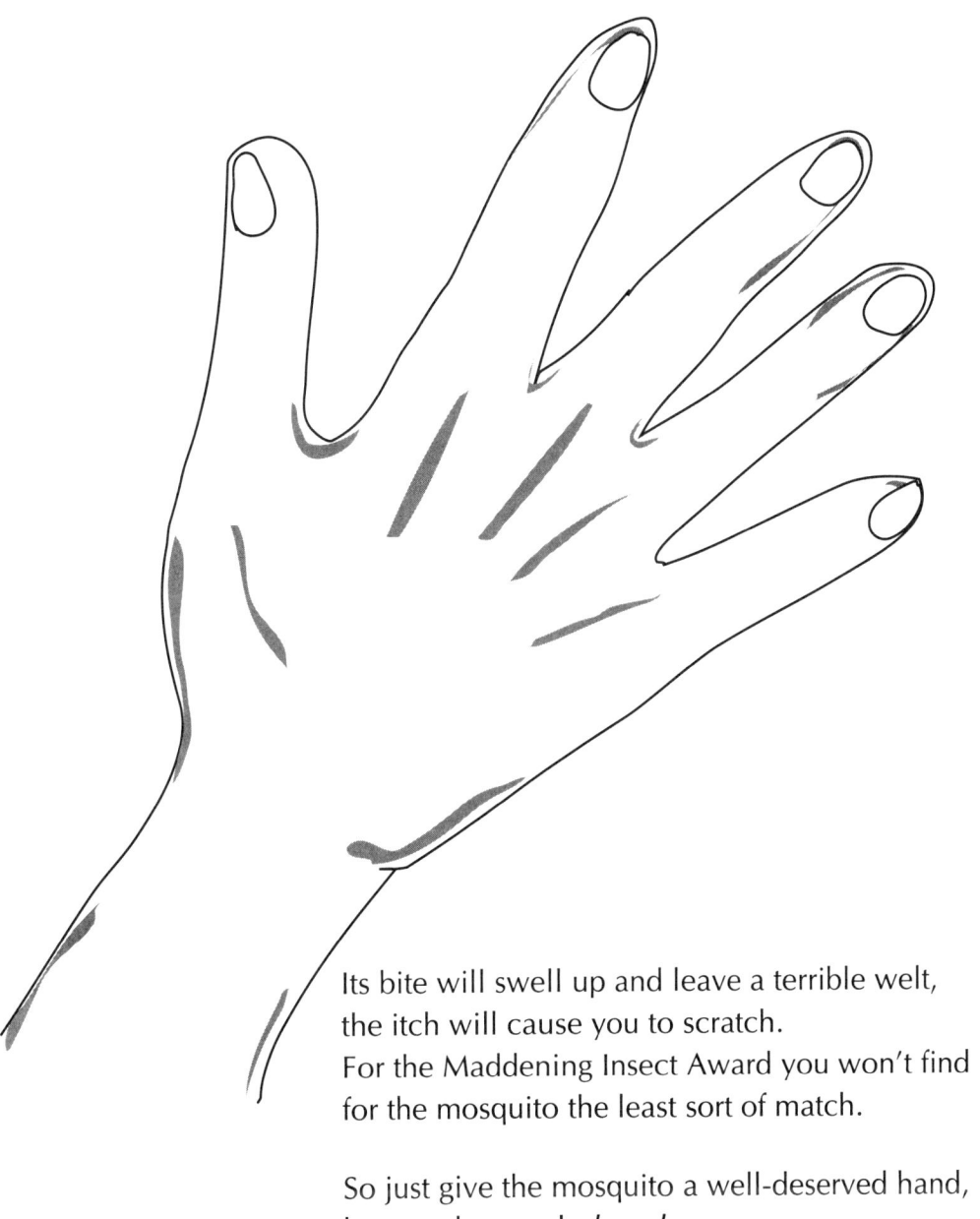

Its bite will swell up and leave a terrible welt,
the itch will cause you to scratch.
For the Maddening Insect Award you won't find
for the mosquito the least sort of match.

So just give the mosquito a well-deserved hand,
but not the usual *clap-clap*.
The hand for that pest to which I'm referring
is a hard one that's swift and goes "SLAP!"

Oops!

There once was a Russian named Kosov
 Who, while trimming his nails, cut his toes off.
Asked if he missed them, he sighed—
"Not at all," he replied,
"If I lived in Siberia they'd be froze off!"

Bash Bash

Big bully Bill bopped Bob on the beak,
but Bob barely blinked at the blow.
Then Bob brashly battled and bashed Billy back,
Billy's body bruised badly from his brow to his toe.

Both of the boys began to bellow and bray
and belligerently behaved in a bellicose way.
Blow begat bop begat biff begat fray.
—Those boisterous bullies still bicker today!

Adipose, I Suppose

Tommy ate a donut
and then he ate five more;
—ten custard pies, eight Danish rolls
were added to his score.
He gobbled and he swallowed
five pounds of chocolate fudge,
ten ice cream cones, a piece of cake
and Tom could barely budge.
He kept ten bakers baking,
indeed, he paid their salaries,
consuming each and every day
at least ten zillion calories.
Tommy felt his buttons pop,
his pants grew much too tight,
his anatomy was changing—
Tom was quite a sight.
When Tommy looked behind him
his rear was no mere bump,
it looked as though he was endowed
with a hippopotamus's rump.
The doctor took one look at him
and said, "It is my guess
that Tommy is experiencing
the seat-swell of excess!"

Hi, Ho, Sliver...

In the old lumber pile he was playing one day—
my friend Stanley Kevin McClank.
While slipping and sliding his pants ripped away;
he got a splinter from an old rough-hewn plank.

The stinging sensation made Stanley fear,
so he quit everything he was doing.
He knew he was wounded somewhere in the rear
and his pants needed some sewing or gluing.

He ran on home as fast as he could
to seek after some sweet sympathy.
"it's as big as a ten-penny nail, but it's wood,
and it throbs like a bass tympani."

As seconds ticked by, that sliver kept growing,
at least in the depths of his mind.
"Part of the pain is thinking and knowing
I have something wooden and big stuck behind."

"That splinter's not small, it's as large as a stake
and the pain is extremely severe.
It must be the size of a broomstick or rake,
or it could be a fence post in my rear."

Stan doubted his battle with pain he could win
and he cried out with all of his soul—
"At first I thought it was the size of a pin,
now I'm sure I'm impaled by a telephone pole!"

Then Susan Sarah McFlannery stopped by,
(she's the pretty, young girl from next door).
"Stan, how are you feeling?," she said with a sigh
"I heard you were hurt—what's the score?"

"It was just a slight injury," said Stan, "where I sit,
my shorts just need a small patch.
As for me, I can say it hurts not one bit,
it really is only a scratch!"

Space Ace

Harry Q. Hannibal
The Great Human Cannonball
was shot into orbit one day.
With a ka-boom that was loud
he sailed through a cloud
on past where the birds used to play.

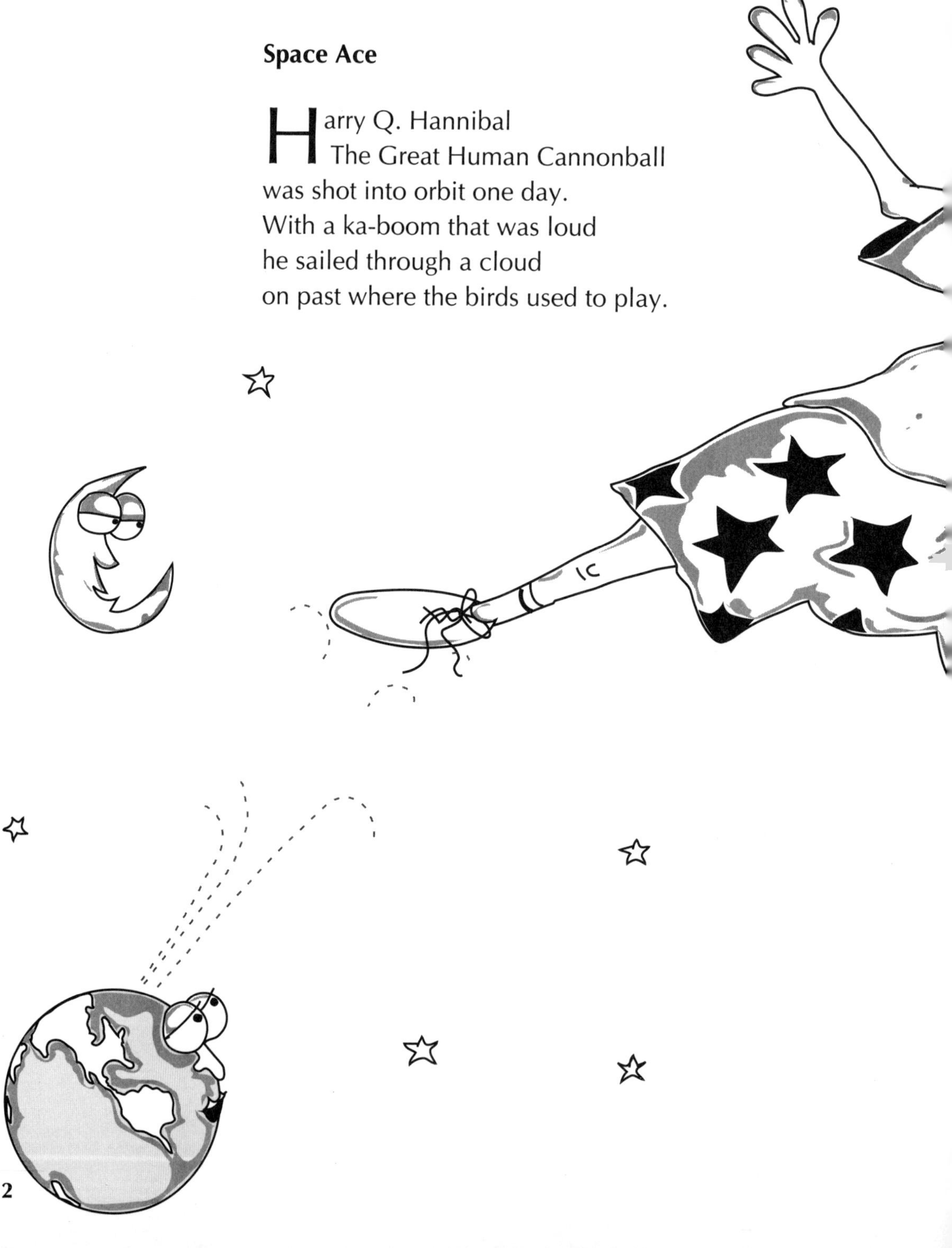

With a grin on his face
he sped out into space
and said, "The view is simply fantastic—
That blue ball is the earth,
I can see its full girth
and the moon's not green cheese— it is plastic!"

An unusual space probe,
he now spins 'round the globe
and orbits it ever so gently.
"The *force* of my fall
I fear not at all—
rather, it's the *heat of re-entry*!"

So low in the sky,
if you look hard and try
to discern him, you might get an inkling
of a light not quite bright
that shows up every night:
Yes, that's our Harry— still twinkling!

Seasoned Athlete

Jeffery Johnson is a winter sports nut
who loves skating and skiing and sliding.
If something's going downhill and it's fast and it's cold,
it is something on which he'll be riding.

On skis he's an ace, a real championship racer;
he's a thrill-seeking, speed-crazed blade jockey
who is at home cutting figures, making spectacular leaps,
as well as winning wild games of ice hockey.

—Although Jeffery's a winter-time wizard,
there is one thing that's really a bummer:
I know he's an expert at bobsled and luge—
But that's winter—and now it is summer!

Whattzit?

With body dark and ugly,
it moves with guile and stealth.
I think that it could likely be
a hazard to one's health.

It has a bunch of hairy legs,
its fangs with venom drip.
Any prey that it might grasp
would die within its grip.

Its features are repulsive,
it's made me a nervous wreck.
I frankly don't know what it is,
but it's crawling up your neck!

A Light Sleeper

When Pirate Pete gets ready for bed,
here's what he does— or so it's said:
He unstraps his leg and takes it off,
removes his chest with a mighty cough,
he unhooks his hook with a grunt and a sigh,
removes his eyepatch; then takes out his *good* eye.
Now, blind in the dark he hops off to bed,
there isn't much there— left of Pete— so it's said.

Yummy!

Cauliflower, broccoli,
parsnips and Brussels sprouts—
headcheese, cow's tongue,
pigs feet, old sauerkrauts.
Limp liver, stewed prunes:
so you want to know,
do I like 'em, do I eat 'em?
No, **no, NO!**

Pizza pie, hamburgers,
ice cream in a dish,
marshmallows, chocolate,
and other things delish—
Peanut butter, popcorn,
marmalade and guess!
Do I like 'em, will I eat 'em?
Yes, **Yes, YES!**

Beak-Speak

A noisy, bold bird—a woodpecker
is eating my Tudor-styled doubledecker.
'though his infernal knocking,
is for bug-larder stocking,
to me he is just a home-wrecker!

Alligators in My Toy Chest

There are alligators in my toy chest—
I know they must be mean.
There are monsters in my attic
that are heard but aren't seen.

Wild dogs hide in my closet,
lurking in the dark.
I often hear them sniffing,
and I think I've heard them bark.

I used to be afraid of stuff
that made noises in the night.
Now I'm brave and strong and tough;
and they give me no fright.

But just to reassure my mom
those things are really gone,
when she tucks me into bed,
I let her leave my night-light on.

Index to Titles

Index to First Lines